SCENE BY SCENE COMPARATIVE WORKBOOKS

FOSTER
by Claire Keegan

Social Setting

Relationships

Hero, Heroine, Villain

Copyright © 2015 by Amy Farrell.

All rights reserved. No part of this publication may be reproduced, distributed or transmitted in any form or by any means, including photocopying, recording, or other electronic or mechanical methods, without the prior written permission of the publisher, except in the case of brief quotations embodied in critical reviews and certain other noncommercial uses permitted by copyright law. For permission requests, write to the publisher, addressed "Attention: Permissions Coordinator," at the address below.

Scene by Scene
11 Millfield, Enniskerry
Wicklow, Ireland.
www.scenebysceneguides.com

orders@scenebyscene.ie

Foster Comparative Workbook OL16 Amy Farrell. —1st ed.
ISBN 978-1-910949-07-8

2016 Ordinary Level Comparative Workbook

'Foster' by Claire Keegan

The modes at Ordinary Level for 2016 are:

Social Setting

This mode refers to the setting and social world of the text.

Consider the roles of men and women, race, religion, social class, etc.

Relationships

This mode refers to the relationships between characters in the story.

Consider whether relationships are difficult, if they make characters happy or unhappy, their importance in the story, etc.

Hero, Heroine, Villain

This mode refers to the study and analysis of a specific lead character.

Consider the character's personality, behavior, what you like and dislike about them, etc.

About This Workbook

Our workbooks are for the Leaving Certificate Comparative Study.

Each workbook is divided into three coloured sections, one for each comparative mode. This makes it easy to identify each mode and make comparisons and contrasts between texts – simply use matching coloured sections of each of your workbooks to identify similarities and differences.

Each coloured section has two parts to it. The first part focuses on the text itself, and asks text-specific questions within a comparative mode. This helps you get familiar with the text and the aspects of the text that are covered by that mode.

The second part of each section focuses on one of the modes. In this part, you are asked more general, mode-specific questions. You then have to take what you know about the text and apply it to the mode. By doing this you will become very familiar with what each mode involves, and it will help prepare you for writing comparative answers.

Once complete, this workbook will become your set of notes, to revise and study before the exam, and to help you when preparing comparative essays for class.

We hope our workbooks help you conquer the comparative!

Best wishes,

The team at Scene by Scene

scenebysceneguides.com

Foster by Claire Keegan
Social Setting

Where does the story take place? Describe the countryside where the action takes place. Use quotes/examples to support your points.

When does the story take place? Use quotes/examples to support your points.

KNOW THE TEXT

Are the girl's parents rich or poor? Give examples.

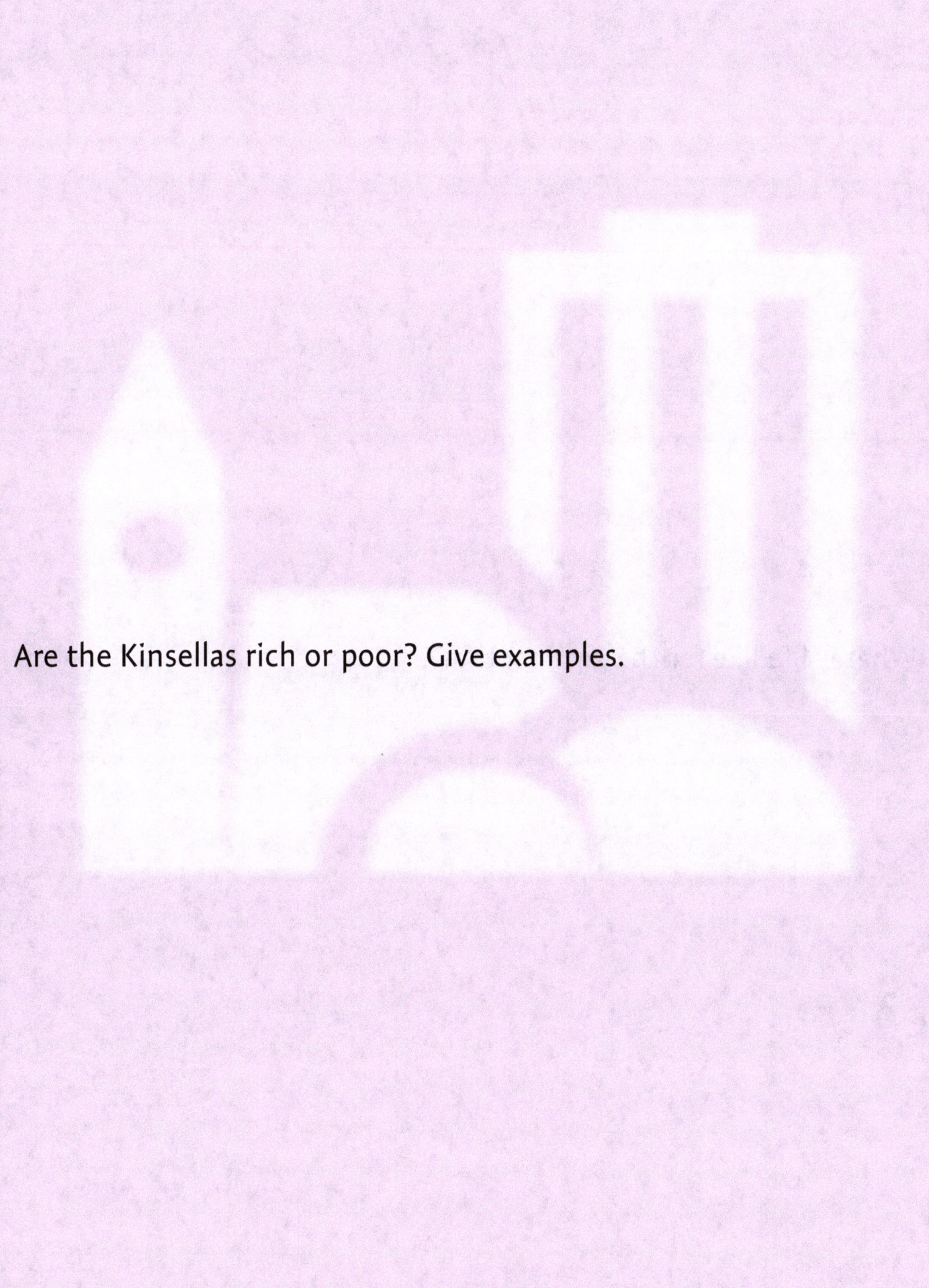

Are the Kinsellas rich or poor? Give examples.

FOSTER - SOCIAL SETTING

How does the girl's father spend his time and money?

What is life like for the girl's mother?

KNOW THE TEXT

How does Kinsella spend his time and money?

What is life like for Edna Kinsella?

How do the people in this story make a living?

What are the Kinsellas' neighbours like? Use quotes/examples to support your points.

KNOW THE TEXT

What sort of person is Mildred, the neighbour who walks the girl home from the wake?

Is it a close-knit **community**? Give examples to support your points.

Are people in this story kind and generous or mean and spiteful? Give examples to support your points.

What does the wake tell you about the **customs** and **traditions** of the people in this novel?

KNOW THE TEXT

Does the girl have any say in who she lives with? Does this surprise you? What does this tell you about the Social Setting of the story?

KNOW THE MODE

Describe the **setting** of this text.

What is the **role of women** in this text?

KNOW THE MODE

What is the **role of men** in this story?

FOSTER - SOCIAL SETTING

How are **children treated** in the world of this story?

KNOW THE MODE

Is **family** important to the characters in this story?

Is **religion** important to the characters in this story?

KNOW THE MODE

Do the characters in this story hold **traditional beliefs**?

FOSTER - SOCIAL SETTING

Is the setting of this text a **violent** or **peaceful** place?

KNOW THE MODE

Is this a **secure** or **dangerous** world?

Where do you see **conflict** in this text?

KNOW THE MODE

How are **characters affected** by the Social Setting of this story?

FOSTER - SOCIAL SETTING

Would you like to live in the world of this text? Why/why not?

KNOW THE MODE

KNOW THE MODE

FOSTER - SOCIAL SETTING

Choose **key moments** from the novel that **highlight the Social Setting** of the text.

KNOW THE MODE

What **similarities** do you notice between the Social Setting of this text and your other comparative texts?

KNOW THE MODE

What **differences** do you notice between the Social Setting of this text and your other comparative texts?

KNOW THE MODE

Foster by Claire Keegan
Relationships

FOSTER - RELATIONSHIPS

Does the girl have a good relationship with her mother?

Does the girl have a good relationship with her father?

Does the girl have a loving family?

KNOW THE TEXT

How do her relationships with her mother and father **change** over the course of the novel?

Are the speaker's parents, good parents?

Why has the girl been sent to live with her aunt and uncle?

Who benefits from this arrangement, the girl or her parents?

Does she miss her parents when she goes to stay with her aunt and uncle? (the Kinsellas)

How well does she get on with her aunt (the woman) and her uncle (the man) at first?

KNOW THE TEXT

How do the Kinsellas treat her when she comes to stay with them?

How do her relationships with the Kinsellas **change** over the course of the novel?

Are the girl's aunt and uncle good foster parents to her?

How do her family treat her when she returns home?

How well do the speaker and her parents **communicate**, interact and understand one another?

How well do the speaker and the Kinsellas **communicate**, interact and understand one another?

KNOW THE TEXT

Do her relationships with her parents bring her happiness?

Do her relationships with the Kinsellas bring her happiness?

Which relationship in the story is the most positive for the girl?

FOSTER - RELATIONSHIPS

Which relationship in the story has the biggest impact on the girl?

What strengths do you see in this relationship?

What weaknesses do you see in this relationship?

KNOW THE TEXT

Do the girl's parents know her well?

Do the girl's aunt and uncle know her well?

Do the girl's parents love her?

FOSTER - RELATIONSHIPS

Do the Kinsellas love the girl?

Does the girl love her parents or 'foster' parents most?

Does the girl's bond with her real family **help or hinder** her?

KNOW THE TEXT

Does it bring her **joy or sadness**?

Does the girl's bond with her new family **help or hinder** her**?**

Does it bring her **joy or sadness**?

In your opinion, which family would the girl be better off with? List your points.

KNOW THE MODE

Are relationships **generally positive** (warm, supportive, nurturing, genuine) or **negative** (cold, cruel, destructive, false) in the novel?

FOSTER- RELATIONSHIPS

What makes relationships in the story **difficult**?

KNOW THE MODE

What would improve relationships in the novel?

FOSTER- RELATIONSHIPS

How do relationships **change** during the novel?

KNOW THE MODE

Does this novel teach us anything about relationships?

FOSTER- RELATIONSHIPS

What is the **most important** relationship in the novel? What makes it so important?

What is the **most important** relationship in the novel? What makes it so important?

KNOW THE MODE

Do relationships in the novel bring characters **happiness** or **unhappiness**?

FOSTER- RELATIONSHIPS

Choose **key moments** from the novel that **highlight Relationships** in the text.

KNOW THE MODE

FOSTER- RELATIONSHIPS

What **similarities** do you notice in the Relationships of this text and your other comparative texts?

KNOW THE MODE

57

FOSTER- RELATIONSHIPS

What **differences** do you notice in the Relationships of this text and your other comparative texts?

KNOW THE MODE

Foster by Claire Keegan
Hero, Heroine, Villain

KNOW THE TEXT

Describe the **heroine** of this novel (the girl, the speaker who narrates the story).

What are her **strengths**? (her good/strong points)

What are her **weaknesses**? (her flaws/weak points)

What **problems** does she face?

KNOW THE TEXT

Does she overcome these problems? Why/why not?

Is the girl **brave** (heroic) in this story? Explain you view.

What confuses the girl in the story?

Why is it difficult for her to solve the things that confuse her?

KNOW THE TEXT

Do you feel sympathy for the girl? Explain your view.

How did the girl change during the course of the story?

What did you **like** about the girl, the central character?

KNOW THE MODE

What did you **dislike** about this character?

Is she an **emotional** character? Use examples to support your view.

KNOW THE MODE

What do you **admire** about the girl?

Is this character a **heroine or villain**? Explain your choice.

KNOW THE MODE

On a scale of one to ten, with one being an extremely heroic character and ten being an evil villain, where would you place the girl? Explain your choice.

Overall, did *you* **like** this character? Explain your opinion.

KNOW THE MODE

Is this character happy or sad?

Would you like to meet this character?

KNOW THE MODE

If you met her, what would you talk about?

FOSTER - HERO, HEROINE, VILLAIN

What advice would you give this character, if you met her?

KNOW THE MODE

Is this character, a 'good' (successful/interesting) main character?

FOSTER - HERO, HEROINE, VILLAIN

Identify the **key moments** in the novel that illustrate the girl's personality/character.

KNOW THE MODE

How is the girl **similar** to the Hero, Heroine, Villain in your other texts?

KNOW THE MODE

How is the girl **different** to the Hero, Heroine, Villain in your other texts?

KNOW THE MODE

www.ingramcontent.com/pod-product-compliance
Lightning Source LLC
Chambersburg PA
CBHW050715090526

44587CB00019B/3387